CHOOSING WINE

ANDREW JEFFORD

CHOOSING WINE

RYLAND
PETERS
& SMALL
LONDON NEW YORK

First published in the United States in 2003
by Ryland Peters & Small, Inc.
519 Broadway, 5th Floor
New York NY10012
www.rylandpeters.com

10 9 8 7 6 5 4 3 2 1

Library of Congress Cataloging-in-Publication Data
Jefford, Andrew.
  Choosing wine / Andrew Jefford.
     p. cm.
Includes index.
  ISBN 1-84172-510-2
  1. Wine and wine making. I. Title.
TP548.J44 2003
  641.2'2--dc21
                                    2003001028

Printed in China

Text adapted from *Wine Tastes Wine Styles* by
Andrew Jefford, also published by Ryland
Peters & Small, Inc.

Designer Catherine Griffin
Senior Editor Clare Double
Production Deborah Wehner
Art Director Gabriella Le Grazie
Publishing Director Alison Starling

contents

fIRST REAd THE LabeL

Wine labels matter. Wine itself, sealed in its bottle, is invisible and mute. The label, therefore, acts as its passport, its calling card, and its welcoming smile. Some labels are beautiful; others are informative; a few (too few) are both. How do you decode them when you're choosing wine?

First of all, look for the name of a grape variety (see pages 10–17). If it is there, that is your best guide to how the wine will taste. If the name of the grape variety isn't there, check the back label as well. Still no grape variety?

In that case, the wine will either come from a recognized European region of origin, or be a non-European wine whose producer doesn't wish to tell you which grape varieties have been used. The next thing to do is to read all the other information on the front and back labels; in many cases, especially with New World wines, this will tell you more about the wine's style and food suitability. The labels may also contain words listed in the Glossary on pages 60–61.

If you are still none the wiser, the chances are that the wine comes from a classic European region: you'll find information about these on pages 18–21, and again in the "Wine Styles" section of the book between pages 30 and 57. These seem complicated at first, but you will soon come to recognize the basic differences, say, between Bordeaux and Chianti, or between white Burgundy and Italian Frascati or Soave. All it needs is a little experimenting—and few experiments are more enjoyable to make than those involving wine.

GRapes anD pLaces

Most wines are made from just one or two major grape varieties. If you get to know these grapes, you'll be able to predict a wine's taste with some accuracy. The soils and climate where the grapes grow also influence their flavor. European producers generally place importance on where a wine is made, while those in Australia, New Zealand, Chile, Argentina, the United States, and South Africa seek to bring out grape characteristics and express their winemaking or blending skills. In these countries, wine is often labeled by grape variety.

key red grape varieties

Cabernet Sauvignon

This is the world's reference red grape. Cabernet Sauvignon travels well and is an exceptional mixer, combining happily with other varieties like Shiraz or Tempranillo. Its flavors mingle appetizingly with those of new oak casks, and bring seriousness and depth to soft red wines. Its home is Bordeaux. California's Cabernets are tannic and grand; Australia's are generally curranty and blend well with Shiraz.

CHARACTER Blackcurrant fruit, earth, havana leaf, dark chocolate, and mint flavors. Cedary, pencil-shaving scents.
KEY REGIONS Perfect in Bordeaux, France; grown wherever red grapes will ripen well, notably in the New World, but also Eastern Europe, Italy, and Spain. For drinkability, Chilean Cabernet is hard to beat. Big California blends age well.

Merlot

Merlot is Bordeaux's most widely planted variety, and the best Bordeaux Merlot is one of the richest reds in the world: soft yet full of fruit. This grape is grown all over the world to make juicy red wines. Hot regions in California, South Africa, and Australia can produce empty, over-alcoholic versions, but cooler areas such as Washington State are already producing Merlots of clearly defined, roundly curranty character.

CHARACTER Dark chocolate (from French oak), plum, blackberry, coffee; savory scents with age.
KEY REGIONS Bordeaux's right bank, especially St Emilion and Pomerol. Also south of France for *vins de pays*, Italy, Switzerland, Eastern Europe, Chile, Argentina, South Africa, Australia, and New Zealand. Big tannic Merlots come from California, with a different charm from the Bordeaux original; Washington State's are softer.

Pinot Noir

The red grape of choice for cool-climate regions in almost every wine-producing country, Pinot Noir makes red burgundy and is used in sparkling-wine blends. Most red wines based on Pinot Noir have light to medium depth of color, a delicate tannin structure, but relatively prominent acidity. Great red burgundy seems to have a lyrical, soaring aromatic character shared by no other red wine—hence its high cost.

CHARACTER Perfumes of cherry and raspberry when young, and more complex, gamey notes with age. Thrillingly vivid, searching flavors including licorice.
KEY REGIONS In France: Champagne, Burgundy, and the Loire Valley; it contributes to many of the best reds of Germany and Switzerland. Outside Europe, cool areas of California (such as Carneros, Russian River Valley, and Sonoma-Green Valley) and New Zealand's Martinborough and Central Otago produce superbly fruited Pinots.

Syrah/Shiraz

In France, this lively grape produces deep black-purple wines, often with strikingly floral scents, vivid acidity, and smooth textures. It also makes balanced blends with varieties such as Grenache and Mourvèdre. In Australia it is known as Shiraz, and Australia's best Shiraz is perhaps the country's finest wine of all: jet black, oil-thick, with dense flavors. It also blends well with the generally stiffer, more currant Cabernet Sauvignon.

CHARACTER Powerful aromas of flowers, cream, hot rubber, blackcurrants, and black pepper. Vigorous flavors, in which early-plum acidity is prominent, include tar, salt, dark chocolate, molasses, and caramel, plus vanilla from careful use of new American oak casks. Syrah's lively style makes it a good mixer.
KEY REGIONS From the northern Rhône valley, but increasingly grown around the world, especially in the rest of France and in Australia.

Grenache

This grape makes appealingly soft reds, light in color and high in alcohol. It's much used for rosé in France and Spain, and creates the sweet fortified wines of Roussillon, too.

CHARACTER Raisiny sweetness of flavor, often coupled with low acidity and ample, soft tannins. Best Grenache-based wines (Châteauneuf-du-Pape, Priorato) have a beefy, spicy character.
KEY REGIONS Grown in southern France, Spain, Sardinia, California, and Australia.

Sangiovese

Sangiovese forms the basis for all Chianti and Brunello di Montalcino. It blends well with grapes such as Cabernet Sauvignon and Merlot, and can support new oak.

CHARACTER Bay leaf, cherry (sweet and bitter), plum, apple, coffee, and leather flavors. Like many Italian reds, it tends to be high in both tannin and acidity.
KEY REGIONS Italy, especially Tuscany and Emilia-Romagna.

Tempranillo

Spain's great red grape, also known as Tinto Roriz or Tinto Fino. It's adaptable, producing both soft and sturdy, tannic wines, and a useful blender, responding well to all types of oak.

CHARACTER In a Rioja or Navarran red, fragrant strawberry flavor and American-oak vanilla scent; from Ribera del Duero, plum-and-chocolate fruit with pencilly tones of French oak.
KEY REGIONS Spain (Rioja, Ribera del Duero, Toro, Navarra, Valdepeñas), Argentina.

Zinfandel

Very ripe Zinfandel can produce wines of alcoholic wealth and sweet richness, and it blends with tougher varieties, too. Zinfandel is also made into a semisweet pink (blush).

CHARACTER Lush blueberry and blackberry flavors. The taste of this grape, though, varies according to the winemaker's methods.
KEY REGIONS This is California's "native" variety—which DNA testing has revealed to be the Primitivo grape of Italy's Puglia.

Cabernet Franc

Makes lighter wines than Cabernet Sauvignon, its offspring. They are fresh and marked by high acidity rather than tannin, with brisk fruit from the Loire, cream from Bordeaux.

CHARACTER Raspberry, currant, or blackberry flavors, which can be mineral-charged. Oak produces pencil-shaving scents typical of "classic claret." **KEY REGIONS** France, mainly central Loire Valley and Bordeaux; northern Italy, New World for "Bordeaux blends."

Gamay

Gamay makes archetypal quaffing wine: low in tannin, high in acidity, stuffed with lip-smacking red fruit, and best drunk young. In a few Beaujolais *crus*, it makes a red wine of deeper flavor.

CHARACTER Bubblegum or banana scents, especially in Beaujolais Nouveau. Red fruit flavors; with age, can start to resemble Pinot Noir. **KEY REGIONS** Closely identified with Beaujolais, but Gamay is also grown in the Loire Valley and Switzerland.

Nebbiolo

A challenging Italian red variety, used to make Barbaresco and Barolo. It provides tannin-laden yet sensual wines of depth and authority, which unfold and soften slowly in the bottle.

CHARACTER Makes lightly colored, powerfully aromatic wine (tar and roses are the classic scents) with complex, persistent, autumnal flavors. **KEY REGIONS** Italy (Piedmont). Nebbiolo has traveled, but not as yet with its Italian grandeur intact.

key white grape varieties

Chardonnay

Most drinkers love this agreeable and amenable grape. Its "international" style has soft, lemony fruit and often the vanillic or toasty character of oak. In Burgundy its styles range from almost austere Chablis to the softer Mâcon and its villages. Other classic Chardonnays come from California, with great substance of flavor, high alcohol levels, and ripe fruit. In Australia, styles range from lush and creamy to poised and bright.

CHARACTER Complex aromas of nuts and butter, toast and cream, wild mushrooms and hedgerow flowers; tastes include lemon, melon, peach, apple, and creamy, nutty, buttery notes. Oak gives this grape a recognizable richness that few other white wines can match.
KEY REGIONS Burgundy is home, but it is planted wherever wine is grown.

Sauvignon Blanc

This distinctive variety is from France's Bordeaux (it is one of the parents of Cabernet Sauvignon). There, combined with Sémillon, it produces subtle, soft, and creamy dry whites in Graves and Pessac-Léognan and the unctuous, amply oaked sweet whites of Sauternes and Barsac. It is much fresher, crunchier, and crisper as a solo performer in the upper Loire Valley in France, and in New Zealand's Marlborough region.

CHARACTER Gives some of the world's most recognizable white wines with the grassy, fresh, zesty, crunchy, stony wines of Sancerre and Pouilly-Fumé. New Zealand's Marlborough provides even more exuberant leafiness, with green sap, gooseberry, asparagus, and zingy lime flavors.
KEY REGIONS Bordeaux, California, Chile, Australia, New Zealand, and South Africa (especially Constantia and Elgin).

Sémillon

An increasingly popular white grape producing richly constituted dry and sweet wines. In Bordeaux, Sémillon is usually blended with Sauvignon Blanc and often Muscadelle; these other varieties add fruit and freshness to its sometimes lumbering corpulence. Australian Semillon is a characterful, pungent, toasty, broad-beamed dry white. Semillon is often, though rather unexcitingly, blended with Chardonnay.

CHARACTER Complex scents (cheese, beans, lime pith, and toast), and flavors of frank breadth. For the sweet wines of Sauternes and Barsac, Sémillon's weight and glycerousness are luscious benefits, especially given the complex flavor added by botrytis.
KEY REGIONS Bordeaux and parts of the New World, most notably Australia (especially New South Wales's Hunter Valley). Other countries' experiments with Semillon have failed to produce wines with much character.

Chenin Blanc

Chenin Blanc can produce wines of extraordinary intensity and grandeur, which can be dry (Savennières, Jasnières, or Vouvray Sec), semisweet (Vouvray or Montlouis Demi-Sec), or sweet, with or without the benefit of botrytis (Vouvray Moelleux, Bonnezeaux, or Quarts de Chaume). Great Chenin Blanc, however, needs a long growing season and careful vinification; when it doesn't get these, the wines can be acidic and coarse.

CHARACTER Aromas and flavors hint at wax, damp straw, pepper, or honey, and in fruit terms at apples, grapes, and apricots in Chenin from the Loire Valley. South Africa's Chenin has a tropical range of fruit flavors quite different from these orchard fruits.
KEY REGIONS At its best in the central part of France's Loire Valley and in South Africa. Huge amounts of Chenin Blanc are also grown in California's Central Valley.

15

Riesling

A peerless, highly aromatic grape, giving finely balanced wines with plenty of sugar and acid; they age superbly. German Rieslings range widely from taut and piercing to rich and spicy.

CHARACTER Riesling's aromas reflect a range of fruits plus honey, minerals, flowers, and (curiously, with age) gasoline. Australian Rieslings have mango, guava, and citrus notes.
KEY REGIONS Germany, Alsace, southern hemisphere, especially Australia.

Gewürztraminer

A pink-skinned grape, usually low in acid. Its best wines are succulent, tight-knit, and rich. New World Gewürztraminers are often impressively spicy, but with rather hollow, tenuous fruit.

CHARACTER The best, from France's Alsace, are rich, heady, almost oily, golden wines trembling with spice, rose, and cold-cream scents and litchi-nut and ginger flavors.
KEY REGIONS Alsace, Germany, Austria, alpine Italy, and Eastern Europe; New World.

Viognier

Condrieu is the "lighthouse" wine made from this low-yielding variety, so extravagantly aromatic it does not need oak. Other varietal Viogniers are slowly improving as the vines age.

CHARACTER Good Condrieu has exotic flower scents (freesia, jasmine, oleander, gardenia). Its ripe peach or apricot fruit is less obvious; its texture deliciously glycerous.
KEY REGIONS Northern Rhône Valley; also Languedoc, California, and Australia.

Marsanne

This rich grape makes fat, glycerous, low-acid wines, which take well to oak. It is used in Hermitage Blanc, combined with Roussanne, and planted in southern France and Australia.

CHARACTER In Hermitage Blanc, it is scented with hedgerow blossom and flavored with white almond. Australian versions have more mango and apricot fruit.
KEY REGIONS Mainly northern Rhône, also southern France and Australia (Victoria).

Muscat

A huge family of vines making wines that taste distinctly grapey. Mostly used to make sweet whites, in Italy it makes refreshing, sweet low-alcohol foaming wines such as Moscato d'Asti.

CHARACTER Makes succulent, sweet white wines, with grape and orange scents and flavors. Muscat always gives a definite grape flavor. Sometimes fermented to give a light, musky, yet dry wine.
KEY REGIONS France, Italy, Australia.

Pinot Gris

Alsace makes the best wines from this grape, from full-bodied dry whites to rich sweet wines. In Italy (as Pinot Grigio) it gives simpler wines. Oregon and New Zealand broaden the range.

CHARACTER Ranges from dry with aromas and flavors of spice, smoke, and bacon, to sweet, luscious, close-textured, pastry-rich, late-harvest wines.
KEY REGIONS Alsace, Germany, Austria, Italy, and Eastern Europe; increasing in the New World, especially in Oregon.

france

These are some of France's key wine regions.

The Loire Valley Chenin Blanc, in Vouvray and Anjou, produces wines of orchardlike fruit. Sauvignon Blanc, in Sancerre and Pouilly-Fumé, has aromas of smoke or flowers. The reds of Chinon, Bourgueil, and Saumur offer pungent raspberry scents.

Alsace Wines, mostly white, are sold by grape variety. Edelzwicker blend, Sylvaner, and Pinot Blanc are quaffers; Riesling, Pinot Gris, Muscat, and Gewürztraminer make deeper wines.

Burgundy Red burgundy varies from light and perfumed, full of redcurrant fruit, to full and sturdy, with black fruit (Pommard, Nuits-St-Georges, Gevrey-Chambertin). In the south lies Beaujolais; its wine, made from Gamay grapes, is juicy and thirst-quenching. In general, white burgundy (made from Chardonnay) is more reliable than red; the best has a varied range of flavors beyond the fruity (including flowers, bread, and nuts). In the north lies Chablis, producing nervier whites.

The Rhône Whites (like Condrieu) based on Viognier are floral and exotic. Those (like Hermitage and Crozes-Hermitage) based on Marsanne and Roussanne are plump, apricot- or peach-suffused. Red Hermitage and Côte Rôtie are perfumed and intense; Châteauneuf-du-Pape is muscular yet sweet-fruited.

Bordeaux Red Bordeaux (known as claret in Britain) has two main styles. Blends dominated by Cabernet Sauvignon, as in the Médoc, are brisk and curranty. Where Merlot is the chief grape, as in St Emilion and Pomerol, the wines have a softer, plummier style. Bordeaux's finest whites are blends of Sémillon and Sauvignon Blanc, giving gently creamy dry wines and unctuously sweet Sauternes and Barsac.

france produces more great wine than any other country

italy, spain, germany

Italy Great Italian red wines rival the best French reds, while its whites are pleasant and food-friendly. Intensely flavored Barbaresco and Barolo from Piedmont are tannic red wines, often with floral scents. Every bit as good are Tuscany's greatest reds like Chianti and Brunello: mid-weight wines with aromas and flavors of plums, raspberries, apples, coffee, bay, and tobacco. Good Valpolicella is light red and packed with cherry fruit, while the best white Soave is richly fruited and chewy. Italy also offers other light, easy-drinking whites like nutty Frascati and Orvieto.

Spain Rioja is Spain's Bordeaux, the home of soft, vanilla-scented, easy-drinking reds. The main grape here is Tempranillo. Navarra's Tempranillo-based reds are similar to Rioja's, but fresher in style. Navarra also produces strong, fruity, Garnacha-based pink wines, *rosados*. Beefy Tempranillo-based reds are also made in Toro and Ribera del Duero, and have deep, vivid plum fruit. From Catalonia comes Cava, a flowery, gentle, and foamy sparkling wine. Sherry is made in the south, in Andalucia.

Germany Fresh fruit flavors and dewy delicacy characterize German wines. The majority of Germany's great wines are made with Riesling grapes and have low alcohol levels, intense fruity acidity, and residual sugar. From the central Rhine Valley come classic wines with rich peach, apricot, nectarine, and orange flavors, and often spicy notes. In the Mosel Valley, wines tend to be lower in alcohol, yet intense with fruit, grass, and leaf scents and an almost explosive grapiness. Nahe's wines are delicate and limpidly flavored, while those of Baden and Franken are richer and drier. German wine presents label-reading challenges. *Trocken* and *Halbtrocken* mean "dry" and "half-dry"; the former can be tart. If neither word is visible, assume a wine will contain some residual sugar.

The United States has three important wine-making states. **California** produces 90 percent of the country's wine. Most is international-style wine made on an industrial scale by big brand names. The best wines, by contrast, are often profound, ambitious, and multilayered, with a terrific alcoholic charge, complex flavors, and ample tannins. (Most successful are the intrinsically rich varietals like Chardonnay, Viognier, Cabernet Sauvignon, and Zinfandel.) The hallmark of the Napa Valley, the most celebrated wine region, is effortless breadth in all its wines, especially big-boned Cabernet Sauvignon and sumptuous Chardonnay.

Oregon and Washington The world's most fickle grape variety, Pinot Noir, is at home in Oregon's unpredictable seasons, and its best wines are true to type, close-textured and complex. Oregon's finest Chardonnays are deft, creamy, and brisk. Washington produces vivid Chardonnay and Cabernet Sauvignon in which relatively high alcohol levels are matched by fresh acidity and fruit flavors; but Merlot performs best of all in this most un-Bordeauxlike region, producing dark, sumptuous, chocolatey wines of thrilling depth and definition.

Chile Vines flourish in Central Chile's Mediterranean-climate zone, perfect for industrial viticulture—yet inexpensive Chilean wines taste more impressive than that description might suggest. Red wines have glorious fruit characters, ripeness, natural balance, and an empathy with oak. This soft, singing quality is Chile's unfair advantage.

Argentina Malbec, Argentina's great red grape, produces thick-textured, earthy wines that can resemble European reds. Cabernet Sauvignon, Merlot, Syrah, Tempranillo, and Bonarda also do well here. Chardonnay and Sauvignon Blanc are improving.

WINE IS
made
IN almost
every
state IN
america

australia, new zealand, south africa

Australia's best wines have a clean, bright stamp to them, and a core of ripe, vivid fruit, the result of pragmatic, professional winemaking and ample sunshine. Australia produces both consistent blends and characterful varietals. In New South Wales, both Semillon and Shiraz produce much-loved and distinctively toasty, tangy wines in the Hunter Valley. In Victoria, the best regions produce fresher, aromatically complex varietals—and great fortified wines or "stickies," too. South Australia is the country's leading wine state in volume and quality, with Coonawarra a fine source of curranty, intense reds with peppery tannic depths. The Barossa Valley is home to black, powerful reds, especially Shiraz. Finally, Western Australia's expensive wines have complex flavors and intense clarity and definition, in particular Margaret River Chardonnay and Cabernet.

new zealand PRODUCeS mouth-shockingly fresh white wines

New Zealand's national style provides vivid, clean, and fresh whites with intense, crisply focused fruit. The Gisborne area produces inexpensive whites; its best are Chardonnay and Gewürztraminer. Hawkes Bay provides top Chardonnays and Sauvignon Blancs with nectarine or greengage flavors, and Marlborough pungent, sometimes leafy Rieslings, Sauvignon Blancs, and Chardonnays. Best reds are perfumed Pinot Noirs from the South Island zones, and Cabernet and Merlot from Waiheke Island near Auckland.

South Africa White grape varieties, especially Chenin Blanc and Colombard, outnumber red, and often have a gently off-dry style. Constantia, Walker Bay, and Elgin can produce crisp and crunchy Sauvignon Blanc full of ripe apple fruit, elegant Chardonnay, and delicate Pinot Noir. Stellenbosch and Paarl are fine locations for deeper reds, including Pinotage, Cabernet Sauvignon, and Merlot.

wine styles

Most of us enjoy wine because of its variety. A lightly grapey Moscato d'Asti is wine; so, too, is a black, thunderous glass of Shiraz. This section celebrates that diversity. Dividing wines into styles allows us to swoop like swallows over wine's entire landscape and make connections which the geographical approach leaves obscure. It's also useful because most of us want to buy a particular style of wine for dinner rather than wine from a precise location or vintage. These pages will provide some ready suggestions.

cReatinG wine's flavors

Nature may create wine's finest aromas and flavors, but careful winemaking can make the difference between the deliciously successful and the sharply unpleasant. The parameters of flavor are set by the grapes: full ripeness, careful hand-harvesting, and rigorous fruit-sorting all count for much.

The winemaker must first convert the grapes' sugar to alcohol (and carbon dioxide) by the action of yeast. This is fermentation. White wines are fermented from pressed grape juice alone, while red wines acquire color, flavor, and textural matter by being fermented with their skins. The subtlest oaked white wines are therefore those that ferment in new oak casks rather than merely spending time in a new cask after fermentation. Cask-fermentation is harder for red wine because the wine needs to soak with its skins, but many top red wines are run into casks to finish fermenting. Simpler oaked flavors can be achieved by adding oak chips or staves to wines as they ferment.

Yeast lees (sediment) which fall from the wine during and after fermentation can also add flavor. Leaving new white wine, in particular, in contact with the lees gives it a subtle creaminess; the lees are sometimes "stirred" into the wine at regular intervals to increase this effect.

Finally, a winemaker may stabilize, fine (make clear), and filter the wine before bottling, to prevent it from fermenting again, clouding, or throwing a deposit when it sits on the shelf. Wines bottled young will usually be fined and filtered so they are bright and deposit-free. Wines bottled after time spent in oak casks tend to be naturally bright and stable, and can be damaged by such treatments. Sediment in all wines, but especially older fine reds, is a promising sign: they have not been over-treated.

Light and medium-bodied reds

It's easy to assume that the darker and more powerful a red wine, the better it will be. Yet light reds play an important role. Most naturally light red wines are grown in northern Europe, and many are made from Pinot Noir grapes, which produce often pale-colored wines with light tannins. As with Beaujolais (made from Gamay), these reds have the texture of a white wine, yet the curranty perfumes and flavors of a red; they are delicious chilled. Italian light red wines include the vivaciously cherry-scented Valpolicella and Bardolino.

The medium-bodied category for red wines is one of huge variety. Plenty more Pinot Noir-based reds, including almost all truly great red burgundies, fall into this category. Their aromas and flavors (of cherry, raspberry, and plum) become complex and savory with age. The best red varietal Pinot Noir (from California, Oregon, cooler parts of Australia, and New Zealand's Martinborough and Otago regions) increasingly mimics this graceful style.

Claret (red Bordeaux) straddles the line between medium- and full-bodied, and here a vintage can make all the difference. In general, less expensive and less "serious" Bordeaux is medium-bodied, and great Bordeaux is usually full-bodied, certainly in its youth. A medium-bodied Bordeaux has ample curranty elegance, complex flavor, and cedary refinement.

Many of the wines of France's northern Rhône Valley are thought to be full-bodied but are in truth medium-bodied; here Syrah grapes give vigorous and vivacious red wines of

MEDIUM - BODIED
BORDeaUX
possesses perfect
BaLance

considerable perfume, yet with high acidity. Other French medium-bodied reds include specialties such as peppery Côtes du Frontonnais and Côtes du Saint-Mont. Bergerac tends to be medium-bodied, with some of Bordeaux's curranty flavor.

Italy has many medium-bodied red wines. Barbera, for example, can be pungently characterful, with lots of raspberry or plum perfume and flavor, always given a fine slicing edge by juicy acidity. Piedmont's lighter Nebbiolo wines are medium-bodied, with relatively pale colors, fragrant scents, tart yet complex flavors, and a dry finish. The deepest forms of Valpolicella, such as Ripasso and Amarone, both fall into this category. Ordinary Chianti will always be medium-bodied.

The majority of reds grown in the southern hemisphere are full-bodied. The chief exceptions are cool-region Pinot Noir-based reds and the red wines of New Zealand. These lively wines are naturally medium-bodied, even though their colors may be dark, with vivid acidity underpinning brisk fruit and moderate tannin levels.

DRINKING notes

FOOD Italy's large variety of medium-bodied red wines, such as Barbera, often have relatively high acidity and some pleasingly bitter back-notes; such wines make exceptionally good food partners, especially for pasta dishes. Chianti's subtle flavors of apple, plum, coffee, and laurel work superbly with Italian food flavors of olive oil, herbs, tomato, and well-seasoned meats.

BEST BOTTLES Great red burgundy will always be medium-bodied. With age, burgundy's fruity aromas and flavors modulate into something complex, savory, even fiery.

EVERYDAY DRINKING Pinot Noir-based wines from France's Jura or Alsace or Germany's Ahr or Baden; Cabernet Franc-based reds from the Loire—try Saumur-Champigny, Chinon, or Bourgueil.

WHY NOT TRY Very pale red wine from Italy's Alto Adige or Germany's Württemberg, made from the Trollinger grape.

TAKE CARE Bordeaux-style blends from North America tend to be frankly full-bodied. New Zealand Cabernets and Merlots can have an unripe streak.

fuLL-bodied Reds

Full-bodied reds are the key wine style for many drinkers.
This puts certain countries at a disadvantage. You'll seldom
drink a truly full-bodied red from Germany, Switzerland,
Austria, Hungary, or New Zealand, while northern France
(like Italy) does not produce full-bodied reds with ease; only
the south is regularly warm enough. Red Bordeaux is full-
bodied in hot years; this means a wine of ample tannin and
intense yet vivid fruit, with the cedary, pencilly scent of French
oak. Rich, meaty, spicy characters are common in Merlot-based
Bordeaux from St Emilion and Pomerol. Cabernet Sauvignon-
based Bordeaux has a sense of restrained amplitude and
textured depth, with blackcurrant flavors when young.

In the Rhône Valley, only the appellations of Hermitage
and Cornas from hot vintages can ever be full-bodied. For
fat, softly full-bodied wine, you have to go south to
Châteauneuf-du-Pape, Languedoc, and Roussillon. The best
vins de pays, made from grapes including Syrah, Mourvèdre,
and Cabernet, can all be full-bodied.

In Spain, modern Riojas have the strawberry-plum fruit of
Tempranillo, shaped by the tannins and toasty, spicy perfumes
of new oak barrels; full-bodied reds from Navarra are similar.
Tempranillo-based wines from Toro and Ribera del Duero are
punchier and more textured than Rioja, with plum notes and
armfuls of oak adding further to the powerhouse style.
Priorato, finally, is decidedly full-bodied at its best, with exotic
aromas and flavors from spicy-sweet Garnacha-based fruit.

australia's natural vocation is for full-bodied reds

Outside Europe, full-bodied red wines are the norm. The long California summer encourages wines of enormous girth and alcoholic power, built around an impressive core of soft yet peppery berry fruit. Oak adds further layers, as does cellar time: the result is complex aromas and flavors (of tobacco, tree resins, turned earth, and spice). Grape varieties used for full-bodied wines include Cabernet Sauvignon, sweet-fruited Zinfandel, powerful and stewy Petite Sirah and Charbono, savory Syrah, and Merlot. The Merlots and Cabernet Sauvignons of Washington State are full-bodied, dark in color, with great freshness and pungency.

Southern-hemisphere wine-growing environments are perfect for producing generously full-bodied red wines. The differences between countries are those of emphasis and style. Chile tends to produce reds of soft, rounded, supple, juicy fruit; Cabernet Sauvignon and Merlot both produce deliciously accessible, fresh full-bodied reds. Argentina is a complete contrast. Its beefiest, blackest wines, from Mendoza, tend to be made from Malbec, though other grapes are also used. The best have pummeling tannins and mineral flavors. Full-bodied reds from Cafayate are fruitier, with less tannin; from Río Negro they are more supple (look for Merlot).

In South Africa, Cabernet Sauvignon and Pinotage from well-known estates in areas such as Stellenbosch will regularly

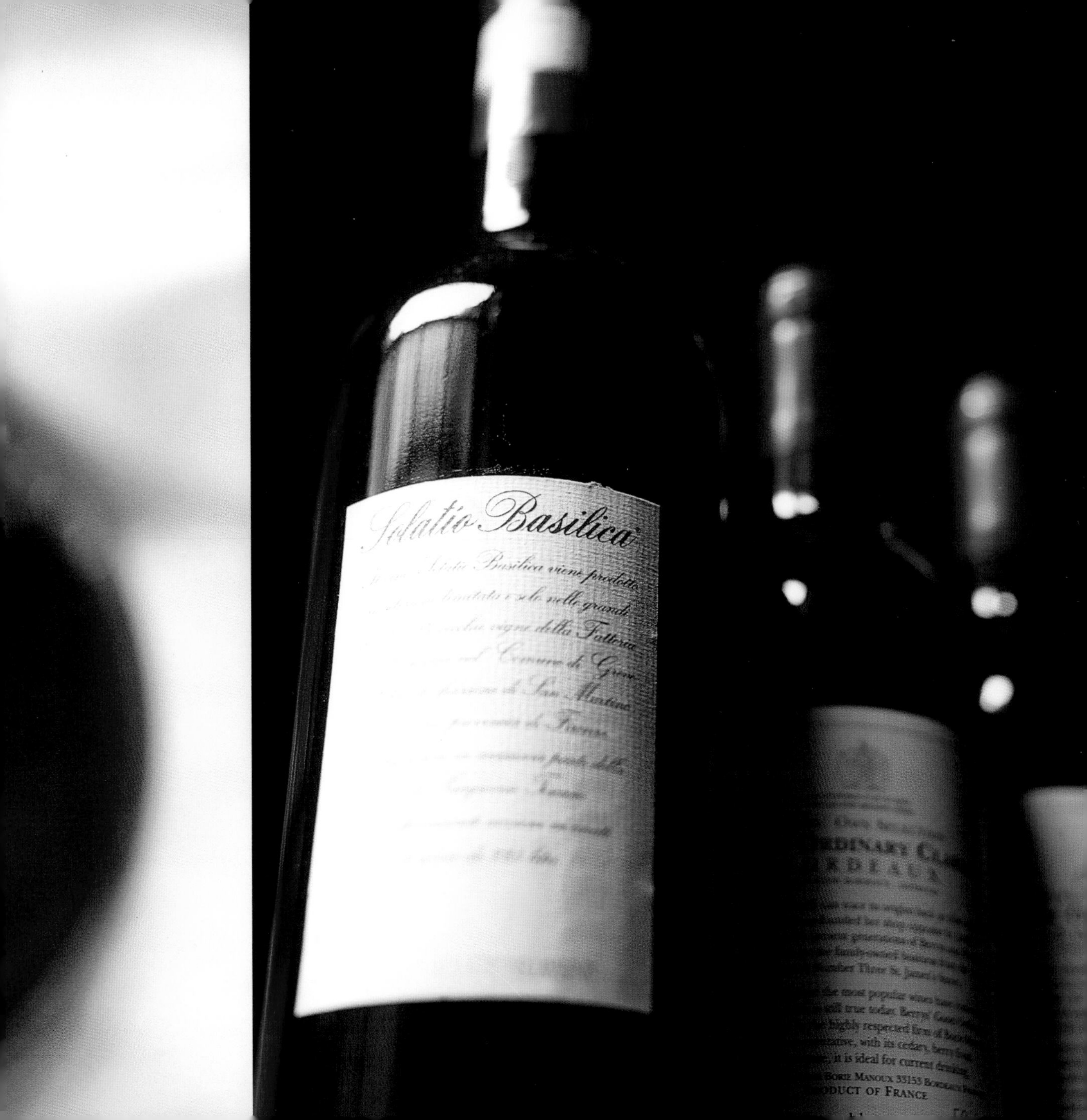
Solatio Basilica
PRODUCT OF FRANCE

DRINKING NOTES

be amply oaked, richly textured, and have resonant, fine-grained fruit flavors. Styles vary from richly fruited, soft, and chewy to pungent, tight, almost roasted wines.

Australia produces a plethora of full-bodied reds with bright, limpid fruit characters and a clean style, often with the sweet sheen of oak. Biggest of all, perhaps, are Shiraz wines from warmer areas such the Barossa Valley or McLaren Vale: these are gutsy, salty, with deep-pile bramble fruit, high alcohol, soft tannins, and fragrant oak. Australian Grenache is rarely as deep in color or richly textured as Shiraz, but may match its sweet-fruited power. Cabernet Sauvignon can be very dark, more freshly fruited, with bright currancy and black-pepper flavors and firm tannins; Coonawarra is the key area for this grape and for Merlot.

FOOD Red meat and red wine have had a love affair for thousands of years; you can't go far wrong, but try to match the biggest, beefiest reds with stews, pies, and fatty meats, and lighter, more graceful reds with plain, lean meats.

BEST BOTTLES Big, bold Shiraz from Australia's Barossa Valley or McLaren Vale; Cabernet Sauvignon from California's Napa Valley; Bordeaux (vintages such as 1989, 1990, 1995, 1998, and 2000).

EVERYDAY DRINKING Argentina, Chile, South Africa, and Australia produce inexpensive full-bodied reds; no country produces more easy-drinking full-bodied red wine than Chile. Bring changes on the full-bodied theme with Australian multivariety blends.

WHY NOT TRY Richly alcoholic, often tarry reds with deep plum-bramble fruit from inland Spain, such as Cariñena, Calatayud, and Jumilla: great value for a winter's night.

TAKE CARE Many full-bodied New World reds are crassly acidified, leading to indigestible "hot and sour" flavors.

Light and medium-bodied dry whites

The driest, flintiest, and sharpest of all dry white wines are produced in Europe. They include brisk, lemony Muscadet; any still wine from the Champagne region; most wines labeled *Trocken* or *Halbtrocken* from Germany; some of the great Sauvignon Blanc wines from the Loire (either varietally labeled, or sold as Sancerre, Pouilly-Fumé, Quincy, Reuilly, and Menetou-Salon) as well as other Loire wines based on Chenin Blanc and labeled *Sec*; and some Chablis. You will also find most plain Bordeaux Sauvignon Blanc to be pungently dry, as is Jurançon Sec. There is an intriguing variety of flavors to be found within this category. Some wines (like Jurançon and Galician Albariño) can offer a spectrum of fruit flavors; some (like Sancerre, Pouilly-Fumé, and Chablis) are stony, flinty, or smoky, with occasional grassy notes; some (like Muscadet *sur lie*) carry a charge of bready flavor from yeast lees. Wines of this sort from the southern hemisphere include those from Tasmania and New Zealand's South Island; both show vivid fruit.

A 349
1997
BOX 548 STELLENBOSCH · 750 T
MULDERBOSCH
STELLENBOSCH WINE OF ORIG

SOUTH AFRICAN
SAUVIGNON
BLANC IS IDEAL
FOR FRESH
SUMMER
SALADS

Medium-bodied dry whites constitute a much broader category. Most wine-producing countries throughout the world make middle-of-the-road whites designed for drinking young with minimum fuss. In Italy, wines in this category include white-almond Frascati, soft pear-fruited Soave, dry Orvieto, supple and fruity Lugana, and gently vegetal Gavi. In France, much lesser white burgundy falls into this category, and many of these wines (like a well-made Mâcon-Villages) offer some of the best value from the country. Medium-bodied, plumply fruited white wines also form the core offering in Alsace, with grape varieties providing variations in style and weight of flavor. Riesling-based wines are purest and most mineral, while Pinot Gris and Gewürztraminer often pass across into spicy, rich, and full-bodied territory. Farther south, many white wines produced in the Languedoc are, perhaps surprisingly, medium-bodied rather than full-bodied: the typical Chardonnay Vin de Pays d'Oc is a lighter, fresher, and more elegant wine than the average California or Australian Chardonnay. Spain's Rueda, Somontano, and Penedès whites are all medium-bodied. Finally, the climates of Hungary, Bulgaria, and Romania give medium-bodied white wines, too.

In North America, Oregon's Pinot Gris and Chardonnay wines are naturally medium-bodied, while the sunnier conditions of Washington State give much brighter, more vividly flavored whites, though without the weight of California versions. Canada's dry white wines, too, are medium-bodied.

The great medium-bodied white wines of the southern hemisphere include many of those made from Sauvignon Blanc and Riesling, and white wines in general which are bottled without any oak influence. Among the most successful of these are, of course, New Zealand Sauvignon Blancs, from the

sample the PUNGENCY AND CRISP edge of a BRACING glass of WHITE

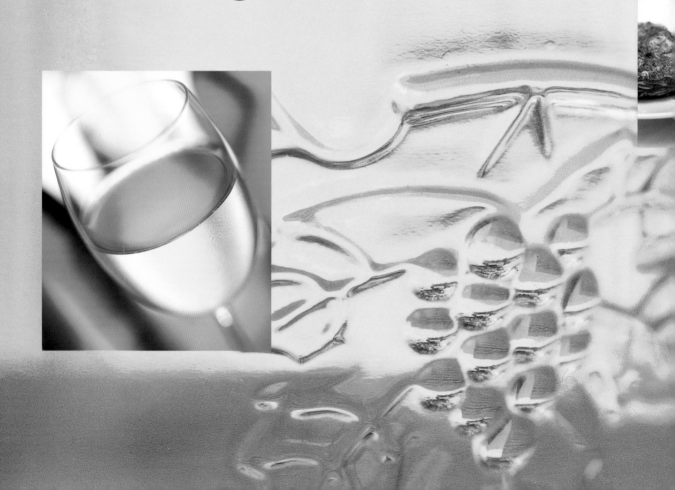

DRINKING notes

Marlborough region, Hawkes Bay, and other parts of the country. Australia's key medium-bodied whites include some of its Chardonnays from cooler-climate sites such as the Mornington Peninsula and the Adelaide Hills.

Australian Riesling, too, comes into this category, although it has only recently been taken as seriously as Chardonnay. The best bottles prove conclusively that this is one of the great white-wine styles of the southern hemisphere. Again, fruit flavors are dominant and oak plays no role; in place of the grape, apple, and peach notes of German Riesling, you'll find a broader, tropical spectrum of fruit (lime, guava, mango) backed by alcohol levels that make these wines exceptionally food-friendly, particularly toward summer dishes.

FOOD Slender, sharp white wines such as Muscadet are the perfect partner for the raw iodine charge of a fresh oyster and its marine juices, as well as for other seafood and fish; they also make invigorating aperitif wines. Italian white wine—nearly always made to be drunk with food—is a sound choice, particularly Frascati or Soave, both adaptable food partners.

BEST BOTTLES Sauvignon Blanc from the Loire (Sancerre, Pouilly-Fumé, Quincy, Reuilly, and Menetou-Salon) or Marlborough.

EVERYDAY DRINKING Lesser white Burgundy from France, such as Mâcon-Villages. Hungarian medium-bodied whites can be characterful and inexpensive.

WHY NOT TRY True Portuguese Vinho Verde, pungently dry with appley slenderness. Beware, much is sweetened for export.

TAKE CARE Cheap wines in this category can often be unpalatably thin and sharp; buy the best you can afford.

fuLL-BODieD DRY WHites

Most full-bodied dry white wines would, I suspect, be burgundy if they could. A great white burgundy from a good vintage is a magnificent drink: structured, nuanced, allusive, nutty, and lemony. Lavishly oaked Chardonnay is so popular around the world because it mimics the profile of well-aged white burgundy—without having to be aged first.

France's other full-bodied white wines include the best white Bordeaux from Pessac-Léognan and Graves. These dry, oaked blends of Sémillon and Sauvignon Blanc also need time to ripen. They are creamier than much white burgundy, with soft apple and citrus notes. The Rhône Valley produces fine wines of similar weight and subtlety. Ordinary white Rhône is plump, low in acid, with soft, muted summer-fruit flavors. The best comes in three guises: Hermitage and Crozes-Hermitage, sumptuously scented with white flowers; Châteauneuf-du-Pape, lush, fat, and glycerous; and finally Condrieu, profoundly floral, unctuous, headily aromatic, richly flavored, and needing no aging. White Spanish Rioja and fine oaked Chardonnay from Costers del Segre (Spain) and Tuscany can rival these.

California produces full-bodied dry white wines high in alcohol and low in acidity, with ripe summer fruit flavors and a happy relationship with oak. Chardonnay is the most celebrated and widely grown variety, often with more than 14 percent alcohol by volume and lushly peachy fruit. Viognier is increasingly grown here, too, and produces alcoholic blockbuster wines marked by exotic floral scents.

GOOD WHITE BURGUNDY
NEEDS AGE; IN YOUTH,
IT IS INARTICULATE

Most southern-hemisphere wine regions are similarly suited to this style. Chile's Chardonnays, for example, are full-bodied and sweet-fruited, with generous alcohol. In South Africa, Chardonnay is grown in warm sites such as Robertson, Stellenbosch, and Paarl, producing wines of creamy flavor.

Australia is famous for its full-bodied, canary-yellow dry white wines. The Hunter Valley's Chardonnay and Semillon wines have pollenlike, honeyed, or toasty aromas and rich, complex flavors. In the Barossa Valley, these wines have a lemony, salty note, while Chardonnay from the Eden and Clare Valleys is fresher. Chardonnay from Coonawarra often has a burnt tang, and from Margaret River, complex, intense flavors.

Other full-bodied dry whites are produced in Australia from Verdelho (with a juicy, tropical character), Marsanne (in a rich, overt, mango-fruit style), and Viognier. Oaked styles of Australian Sauvignon Blanc also tend to be full-bodied.

DRINKING notes

FOOD Full-bodied dry white wines make excellent drinking with barbecued fish and white meats, as well as robust vegetarian dishes and grilled or roasted vegetables.

BEST BOTTLES Great white burgundies from the Côte d'Or villages of Puligny-Montrachet, Chassagne-Montrachet, and Meursault, with their attendant Premiers and Grands Crus. Chardonnay and Viognier from California.

EVERYDAY DRINKING Inexpensive full-bodied white wines such as Chardonnay from Australia, marked by the sunny, melon-and-peach fruit typical of the country.

WHY NOT TRY Broad-beamed, chewy Chardonnays from the Cowra, Padthaway, and McLaren Vale areas of Australia. Also try citrussy Chardonnay from Chile's Casablanca Valley.

TAKE CARE The natural wealth and flavor of California's best dry whites means that some taste almost sweet. Some producers of inexpensive branded white wines will deliberately leave a touch of residual sugar to imitate this.

aromatic and medium-dry whites

Those who know wine cherish its scents; this category is, decidedly, wine's perfumed garden, and the masters of its style the Germans. Great German wine has intense perfumes, low alcohol content, and finely balanced, pure fruit flavors; most classical German wines are medium-dry in style. The Mosel is characterized by flowery or mineral scents, apple and grape notes, and fresh, zingy acidity; the Rheingau and the Nahe tend toward a pure, limpid summer-fruit style; Rheinhessen and the Pfalz are generally richer, softer, and spicier.

Cross into France, and the aromatic theme is maintained in Alsace. Gewürztraminer is one of the world's most aromatic wines; Riesling, Pinot Gris, and Muscat from Alsace can also be intensely scented. The Loire Valley

produces medium-dry Chenin Blanc-based wines labeled *demi-sec* and *moelleux* (the latter slightly sweeter), with scents of damp straw, honeycomb, wax, and orchard fruits.

The delicate white wines of Spain's Galicia tend to be aromatic, though almost all dry; Italy, too, has a small number of scented *abboccato* (semi-dry) wines. Elsewhere in Europe, warmer climates mean that fully dry or fully sweet styles are the norm.

Wines made from aromatic grapes enjoy modest success in southern-hemisphere wine-producing countries, but are generally made in a fully dry or sweet style.

DRINKING notes

FOOD The white styles we've looked at so far include the great food whites, whereas aromatic and medium-dry whites are ideal for enjoying as an aperitif or for *al fresco* drinking.

BEST BOTTLES Fine German Riesling and other aromatic wines from the Mosel, Rheingau, and Nahe areas. The fully dry Condrieu (see page 46) is also astonishingly aromatic.

EVERYDAY DRINKING Gewürztraminer from Alsace. In general, Alsace wines not described as either *vendange tardive* (late harvest) or *sélection des grains nobles* (a selection of botrytis-affected grapes) are medium-dry or dry.

WHY NOT TRY Argentina's "native" aromatic variety, Torrontés: it is easy to mistake this spicy, musky, dry, alcoholic white for a Muscat, though its crisp acidity is often somewhat higher.

TAKE CARE There are many mawkish medium-dry wines made to a formula for cheap sale: pink California "blush" Zinfandel and French Rosé d'Anjou, and German Liebfraumilch, are prime examples.

ROSÉ

This is wine's light-entertainment division. No one wants to pay much for pink wine, so great rosé barely exists as yet. However, there's still plenty of variety.

Many of the deepest rosé wines you can find come from Australia, made from Grenache or Shiraz grapes, with ample fruity flavors. Winemakers in South Africa, Chile, and Argentina generally go for this style, too. France and Spain produce the most interesting dry rosé wines, again frequently made from Grenache (Garnacha). Rosé made in Rioja and Navarra has deep color, plenty of alcoholic backbone, roundly dry fruit flavors, and often a peppery finish. The orange-hued rosés of the southern Rhône Valley in France (such as Lirac and Tavel) are similar.

France makes very pale reds that are almost rosés: Négrette in the Côtes du Frontonnais, Poulsard in the Jura, Gamay in Beaujolais and elsewhere, and Pinot Noir in areas such as Alsace, Champagne (for piercing still red-pinks like Bouzy and Rosé de Riceys), Chablis (Irancy), and the upper Loire. These can be sharp and challenging. The Loire produces excellent rosé; the popularity of the sweet Rosé d'Anjou, however, means these incisive dry wines are hard to find.

BORDeaux makes some of the finest Rosé money can Buy

DRINKING notes

FOOD The ample, juicy fruit flavors of plum-pink Australian rosés are knocking on the door of red wine, and make them ideal for outdoor barbecue drinking.

BEST BOTTLES Bordeaux's fine rosés, often a byproduct of making red wine. To concentrate the flavor of the red, a winemaker "bleeds" off some juice. This *rosé de saignée* (bled pink) echoes the quality of the red wine.

EVERYDAY DRINKING Spanish rosé is usually an excellent buy.

WHY NOT TRY The best dry rosé wines of Provence. These are often now made with subtle barrel-fermentation, to surprisingly successful effect.

TAKE CARE Many pink wines are off-dry or medium-sweet (thanks to a legacy of oversweet commercial rosés); thus perfectly good rosé wine from Chile, say, is often ruined by cloying residual sugar. This is particularly true of California rosés such as the syrupy "blush" (in other words, pink) Zinfandel.

sparKLINg wiNes

In general, the most expensive (and best) sparkling wines come from cool climates, and cheaper (and less ambitious) ones from warm climates. Champagne and sparkling wines are usually dry (*Brut*) or very dry (*Extra Brut*); *Sec*, *Demi-Sec*, and *Doux* indicate steadily sweeter wines.

The leading inexpensive sparkling wines are Spain's Cava and Australia's branded sparkling wines. But while the best Cava struggles to approach the quality of good Champagne, Australia's finest sparkling wines can offer great subtlety and finesse, often based (as much Champagne is) on a blend of Pinot Noir and Chardonnay grapes. The ripeness of their fruit distinguishes them from Champagne.

In Champagne it can be hard to discern fruit flavor at all. Its greatness lies in the fine balance between its barely ripe fruit and the subtle yeast flavors it acquires with age. After many years, mature scents and flavors emerge. The best value Champagnes are those that bear a vintage date.

Sparkling wines are made all over Italy; most common are the low-alcohol, sweet, grapey Moscato versions, while Prosecco is a neutral but refreshing fizz.

DRINKING Notes

FOOD Champagne and other sparkling wines are ideal aperitifs and celebration drinks. They also complement fish and seafood dishes, chicken, and summer fruits.

BEST BOTTLES Vintage Champagne. To gauge how great this can be, try to cellar some for yourself for as long as possible.

EVERYDAY DRINKING Soft and flowery Spanish Cava, with its gentle apple-fruit notes, or the fruity, quaffable, inexpensive sparkling wines from Australia.

WHY NOT TRY Australia produces some superb sparkling red wines, normally based on Shiraz. They seem odd at first, but give them a try: they have unrivaled, fruit-drenched exuberance and vigor, and partner food surprisingly well.

TAKE CARE The cheapest Champagnes are often green and hard, sometimes with a coarse sugary note. Choose a celebration bottle wisely; the most expensive Champagnes are very good, but not twice as good as a Champagne at half the price.

sweet wines

Sweet wines are created with the help of botrytis (see page 60) or by leaving the grapes to dry on the vine or in attics or airy places. The French, Germans, Austrians, and Hungarians are the best exponents of this art.

France's best sweet wines are Sauternes and Barsac. Fruit flavors of lemon, peach, and pineapple are common in Sauternes, while Barsac has a lemony elegance. The Loire Valley also produces botrytized dessert wines made from Chenin Blanc, with an edgier balance and nectarine, peach, and apple flavors. In Alsace, Pinot Gris, Riesling, and Gewürztraminer are often used to make dessert wine. Of these, Riesling should retain its acidity and mineral notes, backed by richer citrus-fruit flavors; Gewürztraminer should offer its scented flavors of rose, litchi-nut, and soft spice more strongly than usual; while Pinot Gris is often richest of all, with sweet, almost tropical fruit flavors.

Germany's sweet wines, categorized *Auslese*, *Beerenauslese*, *Trockenbeerenauslese*, or *Eiswein*, lack prominent alcohol; instead they are dense with fruit flavors and aromas, balancing crystallized fruit sweetness with mouth-freshening acidity. They are, therefore, the least cloying of all sweet wines.

DRINKING notes

FOOD A great dessert wine should really take the place of a dessert, perhaps accompanied by oat crackers and cheese.

BEST BOTTLES Sauternes and Barsac, made just south of Bordeaux, furnish the world benchmark for dessert wines: these luscious, viscous straw-yellow blends of Sémillon and Sauvignon Blanc slowly deepen to a rich gold with time, acquiring layer after layer of extra flavor with each year.

EVERYDAY DRINKING These wines are risky to make, and yields are low, so a good bottle will be expensive; for a cheaper alternative look at fortified Muscats from Spain and France.

WHY NOT TRY Finely poised sweet wine from Hungary, traditionally made in the Tokáji region, with flavors suggesting apricot and apple, dark honey, and autumn leaves.

TAKE CARE German Eiswein has high acidity levels, giving it a slicing edge; only many years' aging will soften it.

storing and serving

Wine's storage needs are darkness (cover racks with blankets), a steady, coolish temperature, and a lack of vibration. A cellar is ideal; substitutes include a cool, darkish cupboard, or beneath a spare bed. Avoid attics, garages, and kitchens; their temperature fluctuations will harm wine.

The ideal wineglass is tulip-shaped, to concentrate a wine's aroma. Thin, uncut glass helps you enjoy and gauge its color better than thick, cut glass; and larger glasses are ideal (to enjoy the aroma, a glass needs to be no more than half-full, which in a small glass can look stingy). Sparkling wines are best served in a tall tulip. A trace of detergent can flatten fizz, so rinse glasses well in hot water after washing.

A wine's serving temperature matters. Most fridges are kept at 4 or 5°C—too cold for all but sweet or sparkling wine. Most white wines are best served at 8°C or so, and richer dry whites (like white burgundy) at 11 or 12°C. Light red wines often need chilling: reds from the Loire and Beaujolais are ideal at 14°C, and even the best red burgundy or Pinot Noir should not be served at more than 16°C. The biggest red wines are ideal at a maximum of 18 or 19°C, so red wine at "room temperature" on a warm summer's day is too hot. Use your fridge intelligently by getting deeply chilled whites out a little while before needed, and putting red wines in for a gentle chill where appropriate.

Oxygenation helps young wines to open up. The best way to do this is to pour the wine into a pitcher, rinse the bottle, and then pour it back into the bottle (opening a bottle to "breathe" has no effect, since so little of the wine is exposed to air). Decanting can freshen up mature or old wine as well as getting rid of any sediment, but take care before rattling the frail bones of an aged red burgundy in a decanter.

Glossary

ABBOCCATO Medium dry.

ABV Alcohol by volume: the amount of alcohol in a wine expressed as a total percentage of the liquid it contains.

ADEGA Portuguese term for cellar or winery.

AOC Abbreviation for *appellation d'origine contrôlée* or "name of controlled origin": French wine coming from an area with unique climate and soil conditions.

AUSLESE German wine, usually medium-dry or sweet, made from late-picked grapes.

AVA American viticultural area.

BARREL-FERMENTED A term used on labels to describe wines which have fermented in wooden casks.

BARRIQUE A small oak cask, usually containing 225 liters (238 quarts).

BEERENAUSLESE Sweet German wine made from grapes affected by botrytis.

BLANC DE BLANCS A white wine made from white grapes alone (in Champagne, from Chardonnay alone).

BLANC DE NOIRS A white wine made from black grapes alone (in Champagne, from Pinot Noir and Pinot Meunier).

BODEGA Spanish term for cellar or winery.

BOTRYTIS A fungal growth on fully ripe fruit that causes dehydration, concentrating sugar levels: nature's way to make sweet wines.

BRUT Dry.

CANTINA Italian term for winery.

CÉPAGE French word for "grape variety."

CLARET British word for red Bordeaux.

CRIANZA Spanish word for wines aged for at least six months in oak casks.

CRU Literally "growth": a French term used to describe a sub-zone, plot of land, or vineyard producing wines of particular interest.

CRU BOURGEOIS A class of Médoc Bordeaux beneath *cru classé*.

CRU CLASSÉ "Classed growth": the top category of red Bordeaux in the Médoc zone.

DEMI-SEC Medium dry.

DO Abbreviation for *denominación de origen*: Spanish term roughly equivalent to France's AOC.

DOC Abbreviation for Italy's *denominazione di origine controllata* and Portugal's *denominação de origem controlada*: both terms are roughly equivalent to France's AOC.

DOCa Abbreviation for *denominación de origen calificada*, a Spanish term indicating a supposedly superior wine to DO.

DOCG This abbreviation is for *denominazione di origine controllata e garantita*, an Italian term indicating a supposedly superior wine to DOC.

DOUX Sweet.

EISWEIN Literally "ice wine": a German term for wine made from naturally frozen grapes, greatly concentrating both acidity and sugar levels.

EXTRACT The substance or matter leached out of red grape skins during fermentation and maceration (soaking), and dissolved in red wines to flavory effect.

FOUDRE A large wooden cask or vat.

GRAN RESERVA Spanish term used to describe wines that have aged for at least two years in cask and three in bottle before sale.

GRAND CRU French term meaning "great growth." Used to describe Burgundy's greatest vineyards, and good vineyards in Alsace, St Emilion, and elsewhere.

HALBTROCKEN Literally "half-dry."

IGT Abbreviation for Italy's *indicazione geografica tipica*, a category falling between DOC and *vino da tavola* (but used for some of Italy's greatest and most innovative wines).

JOVEN Spanish word for young wines without wood aging.

KABINETT A light, elegant German quality wine that varies between dry and off-dry.

LIE See *sur lie*.

MOELLEUX Rich or sweet.

MUST Term used to describe grape juice before it ferments.

NEW WORLD Term used to describe wine production in the U.S., Australia, New Zealand, Chile, Argentina, and South Africa, as opposed to Europe.

NOBLE ROT See botrytis.

OAKED Term meaning that the wine has been subject to some oak influence, generally by being aged in oak barrels, but possibly by having oak chips or oak staves added to it during fermentation.

PREMIER CRU French term meaning "first growth": the top rank among Bordeaux classed growths, but only the second rank in Burgundy.

RESERVA Spanish word for wines that have aged for at least a year in cask and a year in bottle.

SEC Dry (except in Champagne, where it means off-dry).

SUR LIE Literally "on the lees": a French term used to describe wines (such as Muscadet) bottled young and fresh, straight off their yeast lees.

TANNIN The textural component of red wines, extracted from grape skins.

TERROIR French term used to describe the precise combination of climate and soil conditions that creates the basis for wine flavor.

TROCKEN Dry.

TROCKENBEERENAUSLESE A very sweet German wine made from individually selected botrytized grapes.

VARIETAL A term used to describe wine made from one grape variety.

VDQS Abbreviation for *vin délimité de qualité supérieure*, a French term used to denote a wine category lying between AOC and *vin de pays*.

VIN DE PAYS French term meaning "country wine."

VIN DE TABLE French term for table wine: the country's lowest quality category.

VINO DA TAVOLA Italian term for table wine, used (paradoxically) for some top-quality wines.

INDEX

photography credits

FRANCESCA YORKE: Endpapers, pages 1, 2–3, 5 inset, 7, 10 and 11 all insets except below right, 12 insets above, center below, and below, 13 insets above and below, 14 all insets, 15 insets center left and below right, 16 all insets, 17 insets above and center, 26–27, 30, 31, 32, 32–33, 40 center, 42–43, 47 below left and above, 50 below, 52–53, 58, 59 right, 61

ALAN WILLIAMS: Pages 5 main, 6, 6–7, 8–9, 10–11 background, 12–13 background, 14–15 background, 15 inset left above, 16–17 background, 18–25, 28, 29, 30–31 background, 33 right, 34–39, 40 left, 40–41, 41 inset, 42, 43, 44, 45, 46–47, 47 below right, 48, 48–49, 50 above, 50–51, 54 main, 56, 57 right, 59 left, 64

CAROLINE ARBER: Page 12 inset above center **MARTIN BRIGDALE:** Pages 11 inset below right, 17 below **PETER CASSIDY:** Pages 4, 49 right, 54 inset, 55

WILLIAM LINGWOOD: Pages 13 inset center, 15 inset center right, 51 right

JAMES MERRELL: Page 33 center **DAVID MUNNS:** Page 57 left

IAN WALLACE: Page 49 left